Issue #1
Spring 2011

biography
for
beginners

Laurie Lanzen Harris,
Editor

Favorable Impressions

P.O Box 69018
Pleasant Ridge, Michigan 48069

Laurie Lanzen Harris, *Editor and Publisher*
Dan Harris, *Vice President, Marketing*
Catherine Harris, *Copy Editor*

Favorable Impressions
P.O. Box 69018, Pleasant Ridge, Michigan 48069

ISSN 1081-4973

Printed in the United States

Manufactured by Thomson-Shore, Dexter, MI (USA); RMA573AF768, April, 2011

Contents

Preface

Biography for Beginners is a publication designed for young readers ages 6 to 9. It covers the kinds of people young people want to know about — favorite authors, television and sports stars, and world figures.

Biography for Beginners is published two times a year. A one-year subscription includes two 100-page hardbound volumes, published in Spring (May) and Fall (October).

The Plan of the Work

Biography for Beginners is especially created for young readers in a format they can read, understand, and enjoy. Each hardcover issue contains approximately 8 profiles, arranged alphabetically. Each entry provides several illustrations, including photographs of the individual, book covers, illustrations from books, and action shots. Each entry is coded with a symbol that indicates the profession of the person profiled. Boldfaced headings lead readers to information on birth, growing up, school, choosing a career, work life, and home and family. Each entry concludes with an address so that students can write for further information. Web sites are included as available. The length and vocabulary used in each entry, as well as the type size, page size, illustrations, and layout, have been developed with early readers in mind.

Because an early reader's first introduction to biography often comes as part of a unit on a writer like Dr. Seuss, authors are a special focus of *Biography for Beginners*. The authors included in this issue were chosen for their appeal to readers in grades one through four.

There is a broad range of reading abilities in children ages 6 to 9. A book that would appeal to a beginning first-grade reader might not satisfy the needs of an advanced reader finishing the fourth grade. To accommodate the widest range of readers in the age group, *Biography for Beginners* is written at the mid-second grade to third grade reading level. If beginning readers find the content too difficult, the entry could be used as a "read aloud" text, or readers could use the boldfaced headings to focus on parts of a sketch.

Indexes

Each issue of *Biography for Beginners* includes a Name Index, a Subject Index covering occupations and ethnic and minority backgrounds, and a Birthday Index. These indexes cumulate with each issue. The indexes are intended to be used by the young readers themselves, with help from teachers and librarians, and are not as detailed or lengthy as the indexes in works for older children.

Our Advisors

Biography for Beginners was reviewed by an Advisory Board made up of school librarians, public librarians, and reading specialists. Their thoughtful comments and suggestions have been invaluable in developing this publication. Any errors, however, are mine alone. I would like to list the members of the Advisory Board and to thank them again for their efforts.

Nancy Margolin   McDougle Elementary School
                 Chapel Hill, NC

Deb Rothaug   Plainview Old Bethpage Schools
                 Plainview, NY

Laurie Scott   Farmington Hills Community Library
                 Farmington Hills, MI

Joyce Siler   Westridge Elementary School
                 Kansas City, MO

Your Comments Are Welcome

Our goal is to provide accurate, accessible biographical information to early readers. Let us know how you think we're doing. Please write or call me with your comments.

We want to include the people your young readers want to know about. Send me your suggestions to the address below, or to my e-mail address. You can also post suggestions at our website, www.favimp.com. If we include someone you or a young reader suggest, we will send you a free issue, with our compliments, and we'll list your name in the issue in which your suggested profile appears.

And take a look at the next page, where we've listed those libraries and individuals who will be receiving a free copy of this issue for their suggestions.

Acknowledgments

I'd like to thank Dan Harris for superb design, layout, and typesetting; Catherine Harris for editorial assistance; Barry Puckett for research assistance; and Kevin Hayes for production help.

Laurie Harris
Editor, *Biography for Beginners*
P.O. Box 69018
Pleasant Ridge, MI 48069
e-mail: laurieh@favimp.com
URL: http://www.favimp.com

Congratulations

Congratulations to the following individuals and libraries, who are receiving a free copy of *Biography for Beginners*, Spring 2011, for suggesting people who appear in this issue:

Sister Jeanette Adler, Pine Ridge Elementary, Birdseye, IN
Sandra Austin, Tinker Elementary, TAFB, OK
Carolyn Malden, Manito School, Oakland, NJ
Nancy Margolin, McDougle Elementary, Chapel Hill, NC

Louisa May Alcott

1832-1888
American Author and Creator of *Little Women*

LOUISA MAY ALCOTT WAS BORN on November 29, 1832, in Germantown, Pennsylvania. Her parents were Bronson and Abigail Alcott. Bronson was a philosopher and teacher and Abigail was a homemaker. Louisa was the second of four girls. Her sisters were named Anna, Elizabeth, and May. The family moved to Boston, Massachusetts, when Louisa was a baby.

LOUISA MAY ALCOTT GREW UP in a loving family that valued education, hard work, and close family ties.

Louisa and her sisters were very close to their parents and their parents' friends. Her parents were firm believers in several social reforms of their time, and their daughters were raised in those beliefs. They were "abolitionists." That means that they believed that slavery was morally wrong and should be abolished. They also believed in "women's suffrage." That means that they believed that women had the right to vote.

Bronson Alcott belonged to a group of philosophers called the "Transcendentalists." That group included the famous American philosophers Ralph Waldo Emerson and Henry David Thoreau. As a young girl, Louisa read the books in Emerson's library. She also tutored his daughter, Ellen. She went on long nature walks with Thoreau, learning about the natural world around her.

Louisa's mother, called "Marmee," was one of the most important influences in her life. Marmee encouraged Louisa's early talent in writing, and each of the sisters wrote regularly in a journal. Her mother told Louisa "to make observations about our conversations and your own thoughts. It helps you to express them and to understand yourself." Louisa kept her journal throughout her life. She also began to write plays that were performed by her sisters, as well as poems and stories.

When Alcott was growing up, a woman's role was largely limited to being a wife and mother. But Marmee told her girls they could do much more. She encouraged them to become educated, and to choose their own path in life. Louisa's parents also taught their children the value of self-reliance and charity toward others.

Like Jo in *Little Women*, Louisa was a tomboy. She loved to climb trees, run, climb fences, and be outside. "No boy could be my friend till I had beaten him in a race," she said.

The Alcott family lived in many different places while Louisa was growing up. They moved 22 times in 30 years, mostly between Boston and nearby Concord, Massachusetts. The family lived for a short time as part of a community called Fruitlands, but when that failed, they moved again. Finally, in 1857, Bronson Alcott bought a home in Concord, Orchard House, where they lived until 1877.

LOUISA MAY ALCOTT WENT TO SCHOOL at home, educated by her father. He believed that knowledge came from within each individual. For him, the teacher's role was to nurture the love of learning in each student.

Louisa wrote of him, "My father taught in the wise way which unfolds what lies in the child's nature, as a flower blooms, rather than crammed it, like a Strasbourg goose, with more than it could digest."

Unfortunately, Bronson Alcott's theories of education

"Orchard House," Louisa May Alcott's home in Concord, Mass.

were not widely accepted. He wasn't able to make enough money as a teacher, and the family was often quite poor.

GOING TO WORK: Louisa and her sisters began to work as teenagers, to help out the family. "I *will* do something by and by," she claimed. "Don't care what, teach, sew, act, write, anything to help the family. And I'll be rich and famous before I die, see if I won't!"

From the age of 15, Louisa worked at many different jobs, as a teacher, seamstress, and servant. She continued to write, too, and began to sell her poetry and short stories to magazines.

MAKING A LIVING AS A WRITER: Soon, Louisa's income as a writer was enough to support her family. In 1854, her first book, *Flower Fables,* was published.

In 1858, tragedy struck the Alcott family. Louisa's sister Elizabeth died, and the family mourned her loss deeply. Three years later, in 1861, the Civil War began. Louisa wanted to help, so she moved to Washington, D.C. and became a nurse. She wrote letters home to her family about her experiences. These were published as a book, called *Hospital Sketches.* While treating soldiers during the war, Alcott came down with typhoid fever. It left her weakened for the rest of her life.

When the war ended in 1865, Alcott became the editor of a children's magazine called *Merry's Museum.* Then, in 1867, her publisher asked her to write "a book for girls." Alcott wasn't sure she wanted the assignment. "I plod away, though I don't enjoy this sort of thing," she wrote in her journal. "Never liked girls or knew many, other than my sisters. But our queer plays and experiences might be interesting, though I doubt it." That "book for girls" turned out to be *Little Women*, one of the most famous children's books ever written.

LITTLE WOMEN: Alcott wrote *Little Women* in just three months. When it was published, in 1868, it was a sensation. Readers everywhere, young and old, thrilled to the story of the March girls. Alcott based the lives of her

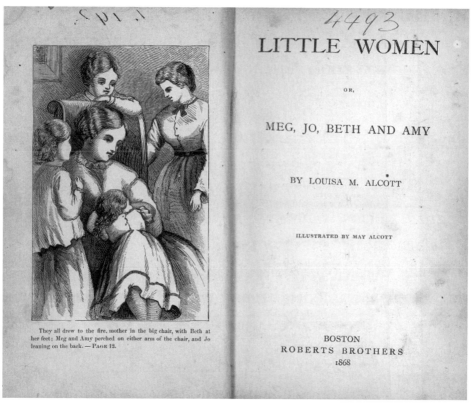

Title page and illustration from the first edition of Little Women.

characters on her own family. She was the model for Jo, Anna appeared as Meg, Elizabeth was Beth, and May was Amy. Bronson and Abigail appear as Mr. March and Marmee.

Much to Alcott's surprise, the world took the March family to their hearts. Readers loved the way each character is depicted as a clear individual. The character of Jo especially was praised as believable in every way. Alcott won acclaim as the first writer to create realistic fiction for young readers. Her eager readers clamored for more.

MORE BOOKS ABOUT THE MARCH FAMILY: Alcott wrote eight more books about the Marches. Known as the *Little Women* series, they include *Little Women, or, Meg, Jo, Beth and Amy, Part Second;, An Old-Fashioned Girl; Little Men; Eight Cousins; Rose in Bloom; Under the Lilacs; Jack and Jill;* and *Jo's Boys and How they Turned Out.* These books follow the March girls as they grow up and have families of their own.

The *Little Women* books made Alcott a famous author. Her books sold so well that her family, at last, no longer had to worry about money. She wrote more books, for children and adults, but none were ever as popular as the *Little Women* series.

Throughout her life, Alcott had devoted herself to social reforms, especially to women's rights and women's suffrage. She wrote about the topics in newspapers and magazines, and was part of the movement to allow women to register to vote. In 1879, Alcott herself became the first woman in Concord to register to vote.

LOUISA MAY ALCOTT'S HOME AND FAMILY: Alcott never married, and lived her entire life with her family. Though she had no children of her own, she raised two of her sister's children. When May died in 1879, she became the guardian of her daughter Louisa. She also adopted Anna's son John.

Alcott moved her family from Orchard House to Boston in the 1880s. There, she lived with her father and her sisters' children. But her health was failing, and she died in Boston on March 6, 1888, at the age of 56.

Alcott is remembered as the first author to write realistic fiction for young people. Her work has influenced writers, especially women writers, for generations. In the March family, she created some of the most believable and beloved characters in all American literature. They are as alive and lively today as they were when she created them, nearly 150 years ago.

SOME OF LOUISA MAY ALCOTT'S BOOKS:

Little Women

Little Women, or, Meg, Jo, Beth and Amy, Part Second

An Old-Fashioned Girl

Little Men

Eight Cousins

Rose in Bloom

Under the Lilacs

Jack and Jill

Jo's Boys and How they Turned Out.

WORLD WIDE WEB SITES:

http://www.lkwdpl.org/wihohio/alco_lou.htm

http://www.louisamayalcott.org/index.html

Aung San Suu Kyi

1945-
Burmese Political Leader and
Human Rights Activist
Winner of the Nobel Peace Prize

AUNG SAN SUU KYI WAS BORN on June 19, 1945, in Rangoon, Burma. Her name is pronounced "Ong San Soo Chee." Her father was Aung San, who led the movement for independence in Burma. Her mother was Ma Khin Kyi, a nurse. Aung San Suu Kyi was the youngest of three children.

When Aung San Suu Kyi was born, she was named

Suu Kyi. In Burma, there is not a formal family-naming tradition. Instead, parents give each child a personal name. Also, Burmese women do not take their husband's name when they marry. So every person has a very individual name. Suu Kyi added her father's name, Aung San, to her own, to honor him.

AUNG SAN SUU KYI GREW UP in Burma, a nation in Asia that is about the size of Texas. It is bordered by the countries of Thailand, China, Tibet, and India. When Suu Kyi was born, Burma was a British colony. Her father, a general in the Burmese army, led the fight for the country's independence from Britain.

In 1947, Burma became an independent nation. Suu Kyi's father was among a group of leaders who were elected to lead the new country. But tragically, her father and several of the new leaders were assassinated in July 1947. Suu Kyi was just two years old.

AUNG SAN SUU KYI WENT TO SCHOOL in Burma for elementary school. When she was 15, her mother was named Burma's ambassador to India. Suu Kyi moved to India with her mother, and went to high school in the city of New Delhi. She was an excellent student.

Suu Kyi went to college in England, at St. Hugh's College, which is part of Oxford University. She studied economics, politics, and philosophy. While in college, she met her future husband, Michael Aris.

FIRST JOBS: In 1969, Suu Kyi moved to the United States, where she worked for the United Nations for two years. In 1972, she returned to England, where she and Aris got married. They moved to Bhutan, a country in Asia, where Michael was a tutor for the royal family. Suu Kyi worked for the Ministry of Foreign Affairs.

The couple returned to England, where their sons, Alexander and Kim, were born. Suu Kyi continued her work as a scholar.

Aung San Suu Kyi with a crowd of school children in Burma, June 2002.

RETURNING TO BURMA: The lives of Suu Kyi and her family changed forever in April, 1988. She received a call from Burma that her mother had had a stroke. She went to Burma to care for her, at a time when her country was in turmoil.

When Suu Kyi arrived, the Burmese people were protesting against the rule of the current head of the government, General Ne Win. His government was run by the military. It restricted people's freedoms and took away their rights. After months of demonstrations, the general stepped down as the leader of his political party.

The people of Burma wanted Suu Kyi to become the leader of a new movement for democracy. "As my father's daughter, I felt I had a duty to get involved," she

Aung San Suu Kyi at a rally in Mogok in May 2003.

said. She spoke to huge crowds of people, and called for a democratic government.

But the military party responded with brutal force. There were violent demonstrations in which thousands of people were killed. Suu Kyi and her supporters would not give up. They founded a new party, the National League for Democracy.

Suu Kyi traveled all over Burma. She spoke to millions of people and called for peaceful, nonviolent reform and free elections.

UNDER HOUSE ARREST: In July 1989, the government placed Soo Kyi under "house arrest." That meant that she no longer had the freedom to leave her own home. Yet she continued to write and speak on behalf of democracy.

In May 1990, elections were held in Burma. Even though Soo Kyi was still under house arrest, her National League for Democracy won a landslide victory. But the government refused to recognize the election results. The National League for Democracy never was allowed to take office. And Soo Kyi continued to be forced to stay in her home. She was not charged, nor was she allowed a trial.

Despite the government's efforts, Suu Kyi remained a beloved leader of the Burmese people. The story of her struggle spread around the world. The world's leaders spoke out against her continued arrest. They called for the Burmese government to release her.

THE NOBEL PEACE PRIZE: In 1991, Suu Kyi was awarded the Nobel Peace Prize. That is one of the most important honors in the world. It is given each year to an individual who works for peace.

Suu Kyi continued to be held under house arrest. Her husband and sons were allowed to visit, but only for brief periods. In 1995, Suu Kyi was finally allowed to leave her home, but the military government restricted where she could go. When she tried to leave the country by train in 1996, she was not allowed to cross the border.

A FAMILY TRAGEDY: In 1999, Suu Kyi's husband, Michael Aris, learned he had cancer. He tried to visit his wife, but the military government wouldn't let him in the country. Suu Kyi knew that if she left, she would not be allowed to return to her country. Tragically, Michael Aris died of cancer in March 1999.

In 2000, the military party placed Suu Kyi under house arrest again. In 2003, she was imprisoned following a skirmish involving her supporters. The military party in control of Burma (which they call Myanmar) would not let her travel freely or promote democracy. Yet she remained a beloved leader in her country. She continued to speak out against the current government.

FREED: Finally, on November 13, 2010, Suu Kyi was

Aung San Suu Kyi on the day of her release,
Nov. 13, 2010.

released from house arrest. She greeted her many supporters with hope and relief. "Thank you for welcoming me like this," she said. "We haven't seen each other for so long, I have so much to tell you." Whether she will be allowed to travel freely in her own country remains to be seen. But for her loyal supporters, in Burma and around the world, her release was welcomed as a step toward change in her troubled country.

AUNG SAN SUU KYI'S HOME AND FAMILY: Suu Kyi married Michael Aris in 1972. They had two sons, Alexander and Kim. Michael died in 1999. After not seeing her for 10 years, Kim was finally allowed to visit his mother in November, 2010. Alexander also hopes to be reunited with her soon.

Aung San Suu Kyi has become a symbol for peace and freedom all over the world. Her determination to bring democracy to her people through peaceful means has made her a hero to millions.

QUOTE

"The struggle for democracy and human rights in Burma is a struggle for life and dignity."

WORLD WIDE WEB SITES:

http://newsvote.bbc.co.uk/mpapps/pagetools/print/
news.bbc.co.uk/2/hi/asia-pacific/1950505.stm?ad=1

http://nobelprize.org/nobel_prizes/peace/
laureates/1991/kyi-bio.html

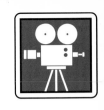

Miranda Cosgrove

1993-
American Actress and Musician
Star of *iCarly*

MIRANDA COSGROVE WAS BORN on May 14, 1993, in Los Angeles, California. Her full name is Miranda Taylor Cosgrove. Her parents are Tom and Chris Cosgrove. Tom owns a dry-cleaning business and Chris is a homemaker. Miranda is an only child.

MIRANDA COSGROVE GREW UP in a suburb of Los Angeles. She got "discovered" at the age of three, when an agent saw her singing and dancing at a food festival.

He thought she was adorable, and showed a lot of talent, too. He talked to her parents, and soon he signed her up to appear in commercials.

STARTING IN SHOW BUSINESS: Miranda started appearing in ads for McDonald's and Mello Yello and also started going on auditions. She landed her first major roles in 2003, at the age of 9. She won a part in the popular movie *School of Rock.* She was also picked for a part on Nickelodeon's *Drake and Josh.*

FIRST ROLES: In *School of Rock*, Miranda played the role of Summer Hathaway, the band manager for the group led by teacher Jack Black. Kids loved the movie, especially Black's outrageous behavior.

DRAKE AND JOSH: In 2003 Miranda began appearing in the Nickelodeon favorite *Drake and Josh.* She played the part of Megan, the little sister. The role really got her noticed. She got parts in other popular shows for kids, including *Zoey 101* and *Unfabulous.* She had a role in the movie *Yours, Mine, and Ours.* And all her hard work and talent helped her to land the part that made her famous: Carly.

ICARLY: In 2007, Miranda started to appear in her own show on Nick, *iCarly.* She plays Carly Shay, who seems like a regular teenager, but is actually the host of her own web show.

The cast of iCarly: Nathan Cress, Miranda Cosgrove, and Jennette McCurdy.

Carly lives with her older brother and guardian, Spencer, in his loft, because her parents are overseas. The show features Carly and her best friends, Sam and Freddie, as they come up with crazy ideas for the web show, called "iCarly." The web show turns out to be a great hit with young fans.

And *iCarly* turned out to be a huge hit with Miranda's young fans, too. It is the top-rated kids' show on Nick, and a great favorite with millions of young viewers. They love the way that Carly is smart, funny, and fun to watch. And kids are encouraged to make their own silly videos, then upload them to the *iCarly* web site. That way, they can be shared with other fans of the show.

MUSIC: Miranda also has a lot of talent as a musician. The voice you hear in the theme song for *iCarly* is Miranda, and she wrote the song, too. "The producer of my show, Dan Schneider, would hear me singing and playing guitar all the time. And he asked if I wanted to try to do

the theme song." She did, and everyone loved it.

The multitalented artist wrote four of the songs that appear on *iCarly— Music from and Inspired by the Hit TV Show*. Her first album, *Sparks Fly*, came

Cosgrove performs for fans on The Today Show, *Sept. 5, 2010.*

out in 2010 and was soon topping the charts.

Miranda's musical career is just taking off, but she's been studying music for a long time. She says that when she was five, she started taking singing lessons. "Then, after *School of Rock*, I started taking guitar lessons. I would always write songs and play them for my friends."

GOING ON TOUR: In 2011, Miranda released an EP that featured her singing with rock legend Rivers Cuomo, from Weezer. She started a tour to promote her new music, performing all over the country for her many fans. She loved it. "It's been a really great experience, getting to be on a bus and going around the United States, seeing all these different places and meeting new people. There's nothing like going on tour."

MAKING MOVIES: Miranda has a growing movie career, too. In 2009, while continuing to work on *iCarly*, she appeared in a movie called *The Wild Stallion*. She plays the part of a girl named Hanna Mills, who visits a horse ranch, where she meets a girl named CJ. The movie combines two of Miranda's loves: horses and acting. She loves to ride horses in her spare time, and working with them in the movie was a great experience.

In 2010, Miranda—actually her voice—appeared in the animated movie *Despicable Me*. She voiced the part of Margo, in a movie that included stars like Steve Carell. She loved making the film, and hopes to do more movies, too.

SCHOOL: Miranda went to public school for elementary school, and then was home-schooled. Now, she has a tutor on the set of her TV show. She does very well in school, and gets straight-As. She is planning on going to college when she turns 18, and is looking forward to it.

ON HER FANS: Miranda loves meeting her many fans. She also knows that she is a role model for many young girls who watch her show. "I feel aware of it when I'm

Cosgrove in a scene from iCarly.

reading scripts," she says. "I want to be able to make things that the people who watch my show can see and that they would enjoy."

FUTURE PLANS: Miranda hopes to appear as Carly as long as she can. "I've been doing the show for such a long time, and I definitely do think about the fact that I'm getting older. At the same time, people still enjoy it. I guess as long as people like it and enjoy watching it, I wouldn't mind doing it. I have a great time."

HOME AND FAMILY: Miranda lives at home with her Mom and Dad, in the house she grew up in. Her parents have tried to give her a normal childhood, and she says she's a pretty typical teenager. "My room is never clean," she says. "I play Guitar Hero all the time and throw things around my room. I'm like the fastest texter in the entire world."

Miranda is an incredibly busy person right now, with TV, film, music, and touring. When she does have free time, she likes hanging out with her friends from elementary school. She also likes horseback riding and shopping for vintage clothes.

SOME OF MIRANDA COSGROVE'S CREDITS:
Television:
Drake and Josh
iCarly

Movies:

School of Rock

Yours, Mine, and Ours

The Wild Stallion

Despicable Me

Recordings:

iCarly—Music from and Inspired by the Hit TV Show

Sparks Fly

QUOTE

"*iCarly* is like a big family. We know each other so well. It's really comfortable, and it's really fun."

FOR MORE INFORMATION ABOUT MIRANDA COSGROVE:

Write: Nickelodeon
1515 Broadway 44 Floor
New York, NY 10036

WORLD WIDE WEB SITES:

http://www.mirandacosgroveofficial.com/us/home

http://www.icarly.com/

Aaron Rodgers

1983-
American Professional Football Player
with the Green Bay Packers
Most Valuable Player of the 2011 Super Bowl

AARON RODGERS WAS BORN on December 2, 1983, in
Chico, California. His parents are Darla and Ed Rodgers.
Darla is a homemaker and Ed is a chiropractor. Aaron has
an older brother, Luke, and a younger brother, Jordan.

AARON RODGERS GREW UP loving to play sports.
He played soccer, baseball, and basketball, but his real
love was football. Family legend has it that Aaron was

34

watching pro football on TV at two. By the age of five he would update players' statistics on his football cards while watching games. His favorite pro football team was the San Francisco 49ers.

He was a great football player from an early age, and his neighbors remember him well. One says she never had to worry about Aaron throwing a football through her window. That's because she saw him throw the ball over her three-story house, and right into her swimming pool, just like he promised he would.

AARON RODGERS WENT TO SCHOOL in California and Oregon. When his family moved to Beaverton, Oregon, so his Dad could go to chiropractor school, he attended Vose Elementary and Whitford Middle School. After his dad finished his degree, the Rodgers family moved back to Chico, where Aaron attended Pleasant Valley High School.

Aaron was an outstanding student and a great athlete. He played quarterback on the Pleasant Valley High School team during his junior and senior years. During his junior year, he passed for a total of more than 2,000 yards, an incredible achievement for a high school player. In his senior year, he set several school records, passing for over 2,300 yards and throwing six touchdowns in a single game.

Rodgers in a "got milk?" ad.

Aaron was a champion in the classroom, too. He got A's in most of his courses, and had outstanding test scores. But no big college programs were interested in recruiting him. At that time, Aaron was under six feet tall and skinny, not the size of most college quarterbacks. Also, Pleasant Valley did not have a great football team. So after he graduated from high school in 2002, he decided to attend a local school, Butte Community College.

JUNIOR COLLEGE: Butte is in Oroville, California, near Rodgers's home. He was the starting quarterback in his freshman year, and led the team to a record of 10-1. Butte won the division championship that year, and ended the season ranked Number 2 in their division.

Rodgers says he learned a lot from his junior college experience. Like him, the players at Butte weren't elite athletes. They came from all walks of life. "You had guys that had been in construction jobs and grocery store jobs," he said. "Some were bounce-back guys, or, like me, guys who'd been overlooked. Everybody was hungry. Guys were playing for the love of the game." It was a learning experience. "That's where I got my confidence," he claims. "And I've never lost it."

During his year at Butte, the football coach of the University of California watched Rodgers practice, and he was impressed. He offered Aaron an athletic scholarship to play for California, and he accepted.

PLAYING FOR THE UNIVERSITY OF CALIFORNIA:
Rodgers began to play for the University of California
Bears in 2003. He became the starting quarterback in
the fifth game of the season, and the Bears went on to
a 7-3 record. They played in the Insight Bowl that season against Virginia Tech, where Rodgers led the team
to a decisive win, and was named Most Valuable Player
(MVP).

Rodgers and the Bears had a tremendous 2004
season. He led the team to a 10-1 record, and set an
NCAA record for passing. It was the best season for the
Bears in more than 50 years. After the season was over,
Rodgers made a crucial decision. He decided that he
would not finish college. Instead, he wanted to become
a professional football player.

ENTERING THE PROS: Rodgers was expected to be
among the first players chosen in the National Football
League (NFL) "draft" in 2005. The draft is the selection
process in which college players are chosen by teams
from the NFL. There were rumors that Rodgers would
be picked by his favorite team, the San Francisco 49ers.
But they picked someone else instead. Rodgers was
picked by the Green Bay Packers.

PLAYING FOR THE GREEN BAY PACKERS: The Packers
are a legendary team, with many wins to their credit. But
when Rodgers joined, they had a legendary quarterback,

Rodgers scores a touchdown in a playoff game against the Atlanta Falcons, Jan. 15, 2011.

too. Brett Favre had been the QB for years when Rodgers arrived. That meant that he had to spend several years waiting for the chance to prove himself.

Rodgers practiced hard, and learned all he could in his early years with the Packers. He didn't get his chance to start until 2008, when Favre talked about retiring. The team's coaches decided to let Favre go, and give Rodgers the quarterback job.

THE 2008 SEASON: In 2008, Rodgers took the field as

the new quarterback for Green Bay. But he didn't have the support of many fans, because he was replacing Brett Favre, a fan favorite. In fact, he was booed by the fans during the Packers' Family Night scrimmage.

The 2008 season wasn't a great one for the Packers. They won just six games, and lost ten that year. But Rodgers showed what he could do. He threw for a total 4,038 yards that year, with 28 touchdowns.

THE 2009 SEASON: The next season, Rodgers really came into his own. Once again, he threw for more than 4,000 yards, and he led the team to a record of 11-5. That was good enough to get them into the playoffs. They lost in the first round of the playoffs, but it was clear he had improved, and was leading the team in the right direction.

THE 2010 SEASON: Rodgers and the Packers had a great 2010 season. Even though he was sidelined for two games because of concussions, the team rallied to finish the regular season at 10-6. There were key injuries to other players, too, but somehow the Packers survived. And they seemed to get better as the season went on.

Rodgers did an incredible job in the final games of the season. The Packers entered the playoffs as underdogs, but they fought their way to the top. In the first game of the playoffs, Rodgers led the Packers to victory over the

Rodgers throwing a pass in the Super Bowl, Feb. 6, 2011.

Philadelphia Eagles. Next, they played the Atlanta Falcons, and once again, Rodgers's play was outstanding. They beat the Falcons to go on to face the Chicago Bears.

The Packers played the Bears in Chicago, and they beat their rivals on their home field in the game, as Rodgers led Green Bay to a 21-14 victory. Now, it was on to football's championship game.

THE SUPER BOWL: Rodgers and the Packers faced the legendary Pittsburgh Steelers in Super Bowl XLV, which was played in Arlington, Texas.

The Steelers, with one of the finest defenses in football, were favored to win, but the Packers took an early lead in the game, which they never gave up. Still, it was a battle throughout the game. The Steelers were down 21-3 at half time, but came back strong in the second half, closing the score to 31-25 with two minutes to go. But the mixture of the awesome Packer defense, and the quickness and accuracy of Rodgers's passing, was too much for the Steelers.

The Green Bay Packers held on to win, 31-25, with Rodgers passing for 304 yards and throwing three touchdowns. It was the first time that the Packers had won the Super Bowl since 1997.

MVP: Rodgers was named the Most Valuable Player (MVP) of the Super Bowl, and viewers and sports writers

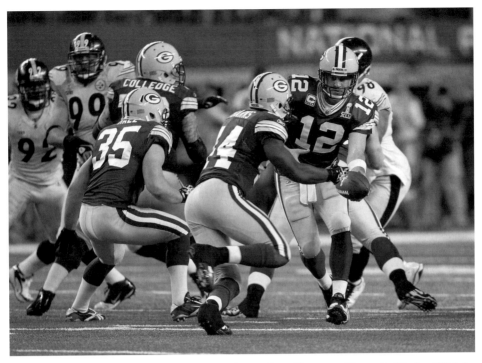

Rodgers handing off the ball in the Super Bowl, Feb. 2011.

all agreed with the choice. Many thought it was one of the finest performances by a quarterback in Super Bowl history.

The next day, Rodgers and his team went to Disneyworld, where they were part of a victory parade. They went home to Green Bay and were greeted by their adoring fans, happy to have the Super Bowl trophy home again.

FUTURE PLANS: Rodgers hopes to play football for many years to come, and to lead his team to many more victories. He's devoted to his team, and works hard to be the best he can be. "I spend a lot of time each week, just making sure I'm ready to play the game," he says. "I want my teammates to know I'm the most prepared guy on the field."

HOME AND FAMILY: Rodgers has a home in Green Bay, but also visits his parents in Chico, California. He is active in several charities, including the Midwest Athletes Against Childhood Cancer Fund. That group raises money to fight cancer in children.

He has also been involved with a Chico charity for years. It's run by the Neighborhood Church, which he attended as a teenager. Every year, he hosts the Aaron Rodgers-Young Life Golf Tournament that raises money for the church's youth group. That group reaches out to at-risk young adults in the community.

QUOTE

When he received the MVP award at the Super Bowl, Rodgers wanted to share the glory:

"Got to give credit to our defense. This is a great group of men that we put together here. It's just great to be able to share it with them."

FOR MORE INFORMATION:

Write: The Green Bay Packers
P.O. Box 10628
Green Bay, WI 54307-0628

WORLD WIDE WEB SITES:

http://www.packers.com/team/roster/Aaron-Rodgers/

http://www.nfl.com/players/aaronrodgers/
profile?id=ROD339293

http://sports.espn.go.com/nfl/players/
profile?playerId=8439

Erin E. Stead

1982-
American Illustrator

Philip C. Stead

1981-
American Author and Illustrator
Creators of *A Sick Day for Amos McGee*,
Winner of the 2011 Caldecott Medal

PHILIP C. STEAD WAS BORN in Dearborn, Michigan, in 1981.

ERIN E. STEAD WAS BORN in Farmington Hills, Michigan, in 1982.

HOW THEY MET: Erin and Philip met in art class at

Divine Child High School in Dearborn, Michigan. Philip was a senior, and very outgoing. Erin was a sophomore, and very shy. He liked her very much, and started asking her out.

"I thought he was making fun of me, for the first month or so," Erin recalls. "But he kept calling, and we started dating that summer."

Phil graduated from high school in 1999, and that fall started college at the University of Michigan in Ann Arbor. He was a great runner, and went to school on an athletic scholarship. Phil studied art at Michigan, and took many creative writing classes, too. As a part time job, he worked at a well-known deli, Zingerman's, where he helped illustrate the catalogs.

Erin graduated from high school in 2001 and went to art school in Baltimore. She and Phil kept up their relationship even though they were apart for several years.

After a year in Baltimore, Erin decided to transfer to an art school in New York City. She also got a job at a legendary children's bookstore in New York called Books of Wonder. She went back to Baltimore to study for a while, then, in 2004, decided to move to Ann Arbor to join Phil.

Phil and Erin got married in 2005, and moved to Brooklyn, New York. There, Phil worked as a freelance illustrator, and got a job at the Brooklyn Children's Museum. Erin worked at Books of Wonder again, then got a job in the children's department at HarperCollins publishers.

The experience of living and working in New York wasn't as positive as they'd hoped. It's very expensive to live in New York, and Erin found it difficult to find the time for her art. But she and Phil were surrounded by supportive friends who encouraged them both.

A friend got Phil an introduction to Neal Porter. He is an editor at Roaring Brook Press, a publisher known for its wonderful children's books. Neal liked Phil's drawings and ideas, and soon Phil had a contract for his first children's book.

CREAMED TUNA FISH AND PEAS ON TOAST: Phil's first book, which he both wrote and illustrated, is *Creamed Tuna Fish and Peas on Toast*. It's based on one of the Stead family legends. In the 1950s, his grandfather, Jack, buried the dish of the title in his family's backyard, because he hated it so much. He even gave the hated dish a gravestone.

The results are hilarious. And any kid who has ever hated one of their Mom's dishes will understand Jack's funny story.

Phil has written about the materials he used to illustrate the book. "The artwork for *Creamed Tuna Fish and*

Peas on Toast [is] collage with acrylics and ink. The collage materials that I use—old postcards, atlases, report cards from the 1930s, shipping manifests, cemetery plot receipts, department store catalogs from the turn of the century, et cetera—come from a handful of junk shops in New York City, Ann Arbor, and Detroit."

HOW *A SICK DAY FOR AMOS MCGEE* CAME TO BE: Phil wanted Erin to get involved with producing a children's book, too. She recently had made a drawing of an elephant and an old man. Without Erin knowing about it, Phil sent the drawing to Neal Porter. Porter loved it. "How can we get her to do a book?" he asked Phil. They planned to get together to talk about it.

Meanwhile, Phil sat down and, within a few hours, wrote out the story for the book. He could see the key elements of the story of the old zookeeper and his animal friends clearly in his mind. He shared the story with Erin, and told her he wanted her to do the illustrations. They started to work on the book, but ran into problems.

The Steads moved to upstate New York, where they thought they could live more cheaply and work more freely. But that was not to be the case. The first week, a tree fell on their car and ruined it. The house they were living in was full of mold. They decided it was time to leave New York.

MOVING BACK TO MICHIGAN: In 2008, Erin and Phil moved back to Michigan. They found an apartment in Ann Arbor, and started to work on the book again.

They were happy to be back, and happy in their work, too. Over the next year, Erin worked on the 32 illustrations that make up *A Sick Day for Amos McGee*. Sometimes one page would take her two weeks. But she wanted the book to be just right. "You want the book to read like a song and you don't want any wrong notes," she says. When they were finally done, they sent the

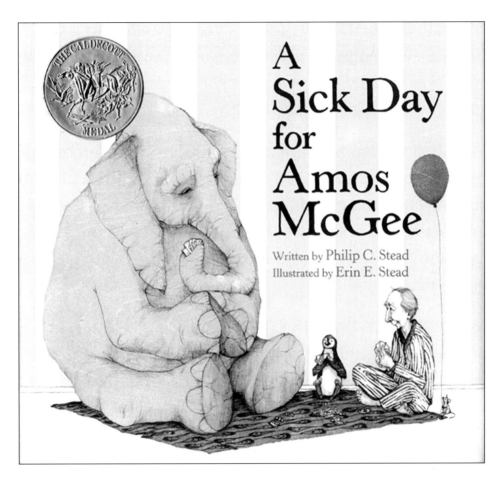

book off to their editor at Roaring Brook, and the book was published in September 2010.

A Sick Day for Amos McGee was an immediate success, with kids and adults, too. They loved the warm and witty story. They also loved the illustrations, with their warm, muted tones, which Erin created with woodblock prints and pencil.

A Sick Day for Amos McGee is about friendship and caring. It features the kindly Amos McGee, the caretaker of a rather remarkable group of zoo animals. They include a chess-playing elephant, a shy penguin, a tortoise who likes to race, a rhinoceros with a runny nose, and an owl who's afraid of the dark.

All of the animals are deeply attached to their loving keeper, so when he gets a cold, they decide to pay him a visit. The zoo animals travel by bus, and when they arrive at Amos's house, he is delighted to see them. They become Amos's caretakers for the day, then snuggle up to spend the night.

WINNING THE CALDECOTT: On January 11, 2011, Erin received a very important phone call from the American Library Association. She learned that she had won the Caldecott Medal for *A Sick Day for Amos McGee*. That's the highest award in children's book illustration.

Erin's a very shy person, and the news was just overwhelming. "I'm not a screamer when I hear good news," she says. "I was speechless." Phil had left to walk the dog, so Erin ran to find him and share the wonderful news.

Soon, the Steads were invited to New York, where they celebrated their good fortune with their publisher. Then, they began a whirlwind tour of the country, giving interviews and meeting with their many fans at libraries and bookstores. They're still amazed at the award, and are very happy to be doing what they love to do.

FUTURE PLANS: Phil has a new book coming out in the Spring of 2011. It's called *Jonathan and the Big Blue Boat.* This is how he describes it: "*Jonathan and the Big Blue Boat* is the story of Jonathan, a little boy who's favorite bear, Frederick, is given away by his surprisingly insensitive parents. Jonathan embarks on a voyage on a big blue steamboat in an effort to recover Frederick. Along the way he meets some unlikely characters—a circus elephant, a mountain goat, a whale—who join him on his search."

"*Jonathan and the Big Blue Boat* is a very personal project for me," Phil says. "I've had a fascination with big ships since I was a child visiting the Great Lakes and watching the freighters on their way to the auto plants in Detroit. When I was ten years old, I began collecting stamps that featured ships in their artwork. I still have them and regularly add to that collection. Many of those stamps have been used in the collage work for Jonathan, or have otherwise inspired certain images."

Jonathan's bear has a personal story, too. "Frederick, the object of Jonathan's search, has been my real bear since Christmas 1984. I took him everywhere as a kid. These days Frederick keeps me company in the studio."

Erin is working on new books, too. She is working on the illustrations for a book written by her friend Julie Fogliano, called *And then It's Spring.* And she and Phil are working on a new book. "Phil has written me another story (!) which I am working on right now," she wrote recently. "It's about a bear and will be out Fall 2012."

HOME AND FAMILY: Erin and Phil live and work in a restored barn near the train station in downtown Ann

Arbor, Michigan. They have a studio that they share on one floor of their home, which has big windows that let in lots of natural light. Phil also works part time as an instructor at Washtenaw Community College in Ann Arbor. They spend most of their time together, and love to take their dog, Wednesday, for long walks.

Erin and Phil work together very well, and they share their work and thoughts with one another. "He's my biggest inspiration and the person I rely on for critiques," Erin says of Phil. "Erin is my first editor," says Phil. "I never do anything without sharing it with her first."

SOME OF ERIN AND PHILIP STEAD'S BOOKS:

Creamed Tuna Fish and Peas on Toast (written and illustrated by Philip Stead)

A Sick Day for Amos McGee (written by Philip Stead and illustrated by Erin Stead)

Jonathan and the Big Blue Boat (written and illustrated by Philip Stead)

FOR MORE INFORMATION:

Write: Roaring Brook Press
175 Fifth Avenue
New York, NY 10010

QUOTE

Recently, Erin said this about being an illustrator:

"I think the best books (the books that Philip and I try very hard to deserve to share shelf space with) aren't necessarily aimed at a younger audience. I think they're just aimed at people. I think it's just as hard to be a kid as it is to be an adult. If you can tug at a person a little (whether they're small or big) and make them feel sincerely happy, or sad, or silly, then that is a real book. The best part for me about being an illustrator is that it keeps me honest. If I can make a book as honest as I can and my book makes someone (small or big) feel something honest, than maybe I have made a real book."

WORLD WIDE WEB SITES:

http://www.philipstead.com/

http://blog.erinstead.com/

http://us.macmillan.com/asickdayforamosmcgee/

Clare Vanderpool

1964-
American Author of Books for Children
Author of *Moon over Manifest*, Winner of the
2011 Newbery Medal

CLARE VANDERPOOL WAS BORN in November 1964, in Wichita, Kansas. Her name when she was born was Clare Sander. Vanderpool became her last name when she married.

CLARE VANDERPOOL GREW UP in the Wichita neighborhood called College Hill, where she still lives today.

From the time she was very small, she loved to read. She claims she even read while in store dressing rooms, math class, and even in church. Her favorite authors when she was little included Scott O'Dell, Madeleine L'Engle, and Elizabeth George Speare. By the time she was 10, Clare had decided she would be an author, too.

She enjoyed a happy home life, and remembers family vacations exploring the country. Even these trips involved reading. On one memorable vacation to Canada's Prince Edward Island, Clare's mother read to her from *Anne of Green Gables*. That's Lucy Maud Montgomery's book about one of the world's most famous and beloved fictional characters, Anne Shirley.

CLARE VANDERPOOL WENT TO SCHOOL at Blessed Sacrament Catholic School in Wichita for elementary school, then to the Wichita Collegiate School for high school. She attended Newman University in Wichita for college, where she studied English and elementary education.

FIRST JOBS: After graduating from college in 1987, Vanderpool worked for the Wichita Catholic Diocese. There, she was the director of youth ministries. She continued to work after she got married, but decided to be a stay-at-home mom after her children were born.

STARTING TO WRITE FOR KIDS: Vanderpool recalls

that she began writing her award-winning children's book, *Moon over Manifest*, around 2001. By then, she was a busy Mom with four children, ranging in age from one to seven. She jokes that she wrote whenever she could squeeze in a few minutes, "during *Sesame Street*, at long traffic lights, and during church."

It was a busy time for her and her family. "I wasn't sitting around writing all the time. I was also making lunches, driving to field trips, folding laundry, and saying 'Hurry up, you'll be late'."

MOON OVER MANIFEST: Vanderpool's first and only novel for kids so far is *Moon over Manifest*. It takes place during the Great Depression, a time in the 1930s when banks failed, people lost their homes, and more than 25% of Americans couldn't find work.

The central character of the novel is 12-year-old Abilene Tucker. She has spent most of her young years traveling with her father. Like many people during the Depression, they are very poor. Abilene's father works for the railroad, and the two of them ride trains from city to city, with no real home.

As the book begins, Abilene is sent to live with a friend of her fathers, Howard Shady, in Manifest, Kansas, while her father continues to ride the rails. The town of Manifest doesn't exist in real life, but Vanderpool based

it on the real Kansas city of Frontenac, where her grand-parents lived. She says it has a "rich and colorful history" that helped move the action of the story along.

Abilene's story unfolds as she looks into the history of the town, especially as it relates to several mysterious townsfolk who lived in Manifest in 1918, just as the first World War was ending. Throughout the novel, Abilene unravels clues from old newspapers, letters from a World War I soldier, and even the memories of a fortune teller, as she tries to unravel the mystery. And somehow, her father's life is part of all these stories, too.

Vanderpool set the novel at a time of great change in America. In 1918, immigrants were arriving by the thousands in the country, in search of new lives. She places part of her story at Ellis Island, an island in New York City harbor, where millions of immigrants entered the country for the first time.

In her novel, Vanderpool describes how some of the immigrants move to Manifest, when it was a bustling mining town. What happened between then, and the Depression of the 1930s, forms part of the mystery Abilene tries to solve.

Vanderpool got the idea for a novel set in an imaginary place from a line from *Moby Dick*. (That is a famous novel written by 19th-century American author Herman Melville.) It reads: "It is not down in any map; true places never are." The quote inspired her to create a story about a place and time that is rich with historical meaning. She recalls, "I wondered, what would a 'true place' be for someone who has never lived anywhere for more than a few weeks or months at a time? Someone like a young girl on the road during the Depression. Someone like Abilene."

When she was finally done with *Moon over Manifest,* Vanderpool sent it off to several different publishers. She got a few rejections, but finally, Delacorte Press called to say they loved the book. It was published in the fall of 2010, and was an immediate success.

Readers young and old loved Abilene and her story, which is partly a mystery, and partly a story of growing up. And even though Abilene grew up almost 80 years ago, readers find her, and her story, fresh and new.

WINNING THE NEWBERY MEDAL: To Vanderpool's shock and amazement, her first novel won the Newbery Medal in 2011. That's the highest award for a work of young people's fiction. She got the call, from the librarian who is head of the Newbery Committee, early in the morning in January 2011. "My heart started racing," she recalled. When she learned she'd won the medal, she felt "shock, gratitude, and a great urge to jump up and down."

FUTURE PLANS: Vanderpool is already at work on a second novel, about a Kansas boy who's sent to a boarding school in Maine. "His story involves a journey, a quest really," she says. She's pretty far along in the writing, and when she's done, she will begin to edit her work. She calls that phase the "M & M stage (what I tend to eat when I'm staring off into space trying to figure out where the story is going)."

Vanderpool says she loves writing for middle grade readers: "That age group just seems to be the voice and point of view I settle into," she says. She hopes to write for years to come.

HOME AND FAMILY: Vanderpool still lives in College Hill, the neighborhood she grew up in, with her husband, Mark, and four children.

The entire family is going to share in the benefits of Vanderpool's award. They plan to travel together to some of her speaking events over the next year.

Vanderpool and her husband are determined to keep their kids grounded throughout the experience. "Our plan is to enjoy the whole experience, appreciate the gift that it is, and keep things normal at home. In other words, we still shop at Target, nobody gets a cell phone until they're in high school, and you still have to do your jobs—every week! They seemed good with that."

QUOTE

Vanderpool has this advice for kids who want to be writers:

"Make sure you love it, and the only way to make sure is to do it. So shut off the TV, the radio, the iPod, and spend some time writing down your ideas and thoughts. It can be anything: poems, riddles, playing with words. If you want to be a writer, you need to be passionate about it. It takes time and effort, as all things do."

CLARE VANDERPOOL'S BOOKS:

Moon over Manifest

FOR MORE INFORMATION ABOUT CLARE VANDERPOOL:

Write: Delacorte Press
1745 Broadway 10th floor
New York, NY 10019

WORLD WIDE WEB SITES:

http://www.clarevanderpool.com

http://www.randomhouse.com/author/results.
  pperl?authorid=103927

Jacqueline Woodson

1964-
American Author of Books for Children
and Young Adults

JACQUELINE WOODSON WAS BORN on February 12, 1964, in Columbus, Ohio. Her parents are Jack and Mary Ann Woodson. She's one of four children, with two brothers and a sister.

JACQUELINE WOODSON GREW UP in several places. The family moved to Greenville, South Carolina, when she was little. Then, when she was seven, they moved to Brooklyn.

Jacqueline loved to write from a very early age. When she was just three, her sister taught her how to write her name. She remembers that it made her feel powerful. "I just loved the power of that, of being able to put a letter on the page and that letter meaning something."

Soon, she was writing all the time, and on every possible surface. "I remember my uncle catching me writing my name in graffiti on the side of a building. (It was not pretty for me when my mother found out.) I wrote on paper bags and my shoes and denim binders. I chalked stories across sidewalks and penciled tiny tales in notebook margins."

She also loved to read. She read her favorite books over and over again. Some of her favorite authors were Virginia Hamilton and Judy Blume.

From the time she was little, Jacqueline also learned to live in different worlds. She spent summers in South Carolina with her grandparents, who were wealthy. Then she'd go back to Brooklyn and live with her Mom, who was not. She learned to take note of the differences in people, where they came from and what they had.

JACQUELINE WOODSON WENT TO SCHOOL at the local public schools. She remembers that she loved

English class, and "anything to do with writing." She says she was "terrible" at math and science. She liked gym, and "anything that allowed us to dance or jump around."

When Jacqueline was in grade school, she wrote a poem about Martin Luther King Jr. It was so good that no one believed she could have written it. They also didn't believe her because, when she was little, she liked to make up stories. "Not 'Once upon a time' stories," she recalls, "but basically, outright lies. I loved lying and getting away with it! There was something about telling the lie-story and seeing your friends' eyes grow wide with wonder."

Finally, her teachers did believe that she wrote the poem on Dr. King, and it made her quite a celebrity. She remembers she won "a Scrabble game and local acclaim" for the poem.

When she was in the fifth grade, Jacqueline wrote a short story that her teacher really liked. "This is really good," the teacher told her. It was like a ray of sunshine. "I, the skinny girl in the back of the classroom who was always getting into trouble for talking or missed homework assignments — sat up a little straighter, folded my hands on my desk, smiled and began to believe in me."

In high school, Jacqueline was a popular girl and a

cheerleader. But she never really felt she was part of the "cool" kids. "It always felt like I was outside watching and never quite belonging," she recalls. She knew she wanted to be a writer, and what she wanted to write about: "communities that were familiar to me and people that were familiar to me. I wanted to write about communities of color. I wanted to write about girls."

After graduating from high school, Woodson went to college at Adelphi University, which is on Long Island, in New York. She studied English and literature and continued to write, creating short stories, poems, and ideas for longer works.

STARTING TO WRITE FOR KIDS: Woodson graduated from college and continued to study writing in New York while working in publishing. She met an agent, who reviewed an early version of what would become her first book, *Last Summer with Maizon*. Much to her surprise, he told her that he thought it was really a book for children.

It was a revelation for Woodson. She hadn't thought of herself as a children's author. Then she realized that "every time I started telling a story, the protagonist was a young person." She says she remembers feeling that, in many ways, writing for young people "chose" her. She knew right then and there the stories she wanted to tell. She wanted to describe the lives of people who are often ignored by other people, and other writers ,too.

These "invisible" people, especially young girls, minorities, and poor people, became the characters of her books.

"I knew I wanted to write about things that were important to me. I wanted to write about places that were familiar. I wanted to put the people I loved on the page some way and make them feel powerful. I wanted to feel powerful myself. And the way that those stories came into the world were through the mouths and the eyes and the ears of young people."

One of Woodson's early jobs was as a therapist for runaway and homeless young people in Harlem, New York. Their stories and their experiences in life were a huge influence on her. "I came home with the young people and their problems in my head and couldn't shake the impact they had on me and the impact the world had on them."

Woodson began a career that has made her a favorite with readers from elementary school to high school.

She writes about the lives of children who are very different from those found in most books for young readers. Most of her characters are African-American, and many come from homes where they must face harsh, upsetting things, like the death of a beloved parent. Woodson writes about all these things with great feeling and respect for her young readers.

LAST SUMMER WITH MAIZON: Woodson's first book for young readers was *Last Summer with Maizon*. It tells the story of Maizon and Margaret, who are best friends. They live in Brooklyn, and share all the special things friends do. Then, everything changes. Margaret's father dies. Maizon is sent away to boarding school. Woodson writes about the changes that take place in both girls' lives, as they try to deal with their separation.

Maizon and Margaret return in two more books by Woodson, *Maizon at Blue Hill* and *Between Maizon and Palmetto*. These books continue the story of the two friends, and all the challenges they face. They became favorites with young readers all over the country.

LOCOMOTION: In 2003, Woodson published *Locomotion*. It's the story of a young African-American boy, Lonnie C. Motion. When he was seven, Lonnie's Mom died. It was a terrible time for him as he and his sister Lili were put into separate foster homes.

The book begins when Lonnie is eleven. He's still living in foster care. He's still grieving for his Mom. But Lonnie learns to be strong. The book is a collection of Lonnie's poems, which he writes to tell the world his story. Encouraged by his teacher, Ms. Marcus, Lonnie grows into a wonderful poet, with poems full of life, and truth.

Locomotion was a favorite with many readers. Woodson brought Lonnie back in another book, *Peace, Locomotion*. It continues the story of Lonnie's life, and this time the book is a series of letters that Lonnie writes to Lili.

FEATHERS: In 2007, Woodson wrote another book that became a favorite with young readers. *Feathers* tells the story of Frannie, who is an African-American girl in the sixth grade. One day, a new student, a white boy with long hair who the kids call "Jesus Boy," joins the class.

The class is studying poetry, and Frannie is especially touched by a poem by Emily Dickinson, a 19th century American poet. "Hope is the thing with feathers," the poem begins. Frannie explores the meaning of both "hope" and "feathers" in the book. She learns much about them, and about herself, too.

VISITING DAY: Woodson has also written picture books for young readers. One of them, *Visiting Day*, is about a topic not often found in children's books. It tells the story of a little girl whose father is in prison. She and

her grandmother take the bus to see him on "visiting day." Woodson shows the deep love that the father and child have for one another. It is a moving book, about hope and the meaning of family.

COMING ON HOME SOON: Woodson continues her books about family with *Coming On Home Soon*. It takes place during World War II, in the 1940s. During the war, many men left to fight, and women took jobs in factories in big cities. The book tells the story of Ada Ruth, whose Mama leaves her with her grandmother to take a job in Chicago. The book relates how sad and scared Ada Ruth is, waiting for word from her mother. She knows her mother loves her, but she misses her so much. A season passes, and word that her Mama is "coming on home soon" reaches the little girl.

SHOW WAY: In *Show Way*, Woodson pays tribute to African-American families everywhere. It is a story that starts in the early 19th century, when most blacks were slaves. It revolves around the story of Soonie, whose great-grandmother was a slave who was sold away from her own family when she was only seven. All she has of her family is a piece of muslin, needles, and thread. The book traces Soonie's ancestors, describing their bravery, their strength, and their continuing fight to be free, throughout the 19th century, the Civil War, and the end of slavery.

The book then moves on to tell the story of Soonie, her children, and her children's children, who pass on their love of freedom, of stories, and of hope, all the way

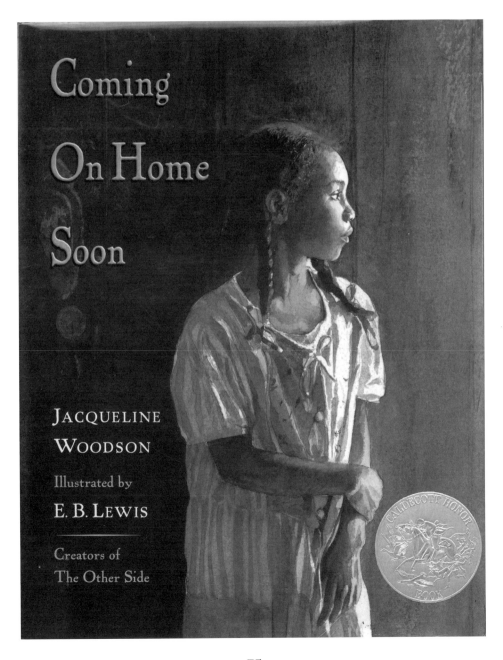

to the present day. *Show Way* is especially about the love that every generation of parents have for their children.

The book is filled with illustrations of quilts, going back generations. Woodson describes how enslaved African-Americans sewed symbols of their dreams of freedom into quilt patches. That is the "Show Way" of the title. Through their quilting, African-Americans could "show the way" to the North, and freedom.

Woodson then describes the history of the civil rights movement in the twentieth century. It is told in words and in pictures of African-American leaders, as well as newspaper clippings that tell of the heroes who fought for equal rights for African-Americans. The final images take the story of Soonie to the present day. It turns out that Soonie was an ancestor of Jacqueline Woodson herself. The final images are of her and her own daughter, Toshi.

Show Way was a great favorite, with readers young and old. Woodson won a Newbery Honor for the book. That is one of the highest awards for the author of a book for young readers.

HOME AND FAMILY: Woodson lives in Brooklyn with her partner and two children, a daughter named Toshi and a son named Jackson-Leroi. She has a writing room in her house, where she works on her books.

ADVICE TO YOUNG AUTHORS: When kids ask Woodson about writing for a living, she tells them, "The way you learn to write is by reading. Read the same books over and over. Study them as you would study a textbook. How does the author get you to feel sad? Angry? Surprised? Turn off your television and write for half an hour. Tell YOUR stories. The world is anxious to hear them!"

She also tells them that writing is hard, but it's also worth the effort. "Anything you do that you want to do well can be difficult at times. Revising is hard. Thinking of new things to write about is hard. And the difficulty makes it that much more rewarding."

SOME OF JACQUELINE WOODSON'S BOOKS FOR CHILDREN:

Picture Books

Martin Luther King, Jr. and His Birthday

We Had a Picnic This Sunday Past

Sweet, Sweet Memory

The Other Side

Visiting Day

Our Gracie Aunt

Coming on Home Soon

Show Way

Pecan Pie Baby

Books for Middle Grade Readers

Last Summer with Maizon

Maizon at Blue Hill

Between Madison and Palmetto

Locomotion

Feathers

Peace, Locomotion

QUOTE

In accepting a recent award, Woodson talked about how grateful she was to the teachers who encouraged her, and the librarians who introduce kids to her books.

"But most of all, I am grateful for young people—young people of African descent and children of all colors. I am grateful when I walk down the street and hear a young person laughing or singing or begging their mom for a few more minutes outside. I am grateful for the little kids in the schools I visit who touch my hair and gaze up at me—curious and open and eager to know something and/or someone different. Curious and open and eager ... to know."

FOR MORE INFORMATION ABOUT JACQUELINE WOODSON:

Write: G. P. Putnam
345 Hudson St.
New York, NY 10014

WORLD WIDE WEB SITES:

http://www.jacquelinewoodson.com/

http://www.penguin.com/youngreaders/

Name Index

Listed below are the names of all individuals who have appeared in *Biography for Beginners*, followed by the issue and year in which they appear.

Subject Index

This index includes subjects, occupations, and ethnic and minority origins for individuals who have appeared in *Biography for Beginners.*

actors

Allen, Tim, Fall '96

Brandy, Fall '96

Bryan, Zachery Ty, Spring '97

Bynes, Amanda, Spring 2005

Burton, LeVar, Spring '98

Cannon, Nick, Spring 2003

Cosgrove, Miranda, Spring 2011

Cyrus, Miley, Fall 2007

Duff, Hilary, Spring 2003

Efron, Zac, Fall 2006

Hart, Melissa Joan, Fall '95

Highmore, Freddie, Fall 2005

Houston, Whitney, Spring '98

Hudgens, Vanessa Anne, Spring 2007

Lewis, Shari, Spring '99

Lloyd, Jake, Fall '99

Muniz, Frankie, Fall 2001

O'Donnell, Rosie, Fall '99

Oleynik, Larisa, Spring '96

Olsen, Ashley, Spring '95

Olsen, Mary-Kate, Spring '95

Radcliffe, Daniel, Spring 2002

Raven, Spring 2004

Smith, Jaden, Fall 2010

Smith, Will, Fall 2000

Thomas, Jonathan Taylor, Fall '95

Watson, Emma, Fall 2004

White, Jaleel, Fall '97

Wilson, Mara, Spring '97

Winfrey, Oprah, Fall 2002

Albanian

Teresa, Mother, Fall '98

animator

Hillenburg, Stephen, Fall 2004

Lasseter, John, Fall 2002

Willems, Mo , Spring 2007

architect

Lin, Maya, Spring 2001

army

Powell, Colin, Spring '96

artists

Caldecott, Randolph, Spring 2009

GrandPré, Mary, Fall 2003

Lin, Maya, Spring 2001

Nechita, Alexandra, Spring 2000

Strug, Kerri, Spring '97

Suzuki, Ichiro, Fall 2003

Swoopes, Sheryl, Spring 2000

Van Dyken, Amy, Spring 2000

Vick, Michael, Spring 2003

White, Charlie, Spring 2010

Wie, Michelle, Spring 2004

Williams, Serena, Fall 2003

Woods, Tiger, Fall '98

Yamaguchi, Kristi, Fall '97

Austrian

Bemelmans, Ludwig, Spring 2004

Australian

Fox, Mem, Fall 2004

Irwin, Steve, Spring 2003

authors

Alcott, Louisa May, Spring 2011

Alder, David, Spring 2009

Aliki, Spring '96

Angelou, Maya, Fall 2006

Applegate, K.A., Spring 2000

Avi, Spring 2003

Babbitt, Natalie, Spring 2006

Bemelmans, Ludwig, Spring 2004

Berenstain, Jan, Fall '95

Berenstain, Stan, Fall, '95

Blume, Judy, Fall '95

Brett, Jan, Spring '95

Bridwell, Norman, Fall '99

Brown, Marc, Spring '98

Brown, Margaret Wise, Spring 2006

Brunhoff, Jean de, Spring 2007

Bunting, Eve, Fall 2001

Burton, Virginia Lee, Spring '97

Byars, Betsy, Fall 2002

Cannon, Janell, Spring '99

Carle, Eric, Spring '95

Carson, Ben, Fall 2003

Carson, Rachel, Spring 2009

Christopher, Matt, Fall '97

Cleary, Beverly, Spring '95

Clements, Andrew, Spring 2005

Cole, Joanna, Fall '95

Collier, Bryan, Spring 2006

Cooney, Barbara, Spring 2001

Crews, Donald, Fall '99

Cronin, Doreen, Fall 2005

Curtis, Christopher Paul, Spring 2000

Dahl, Roald, Fall 2000

Danziger, Paula, Fall 2001

Delton, Judy, Spring 2004

dePaola, Tomie, Spring '98

DiCamillo, Kate, Spring 2005

Birthday Index

3 Jackie Joyner-Kersee (1962)
Patricia MacLachlan (1938)

4 Garrett Morgan (1877)
Dav Pilkey (1966)

5 Mem Fox (1946)
Jake Lloyd (1989)

6 Chris Raschka (1959)

8 Robert Sabuda (1965)

10 Shannon Miller (1977)

11 Diane Dillon (1933)
Virginia Hamilton (1936)
Ezra Jack Keats (1916)

15 Ruth Bader Ginsburg (1933)

16 Shaquille O'Neal (1972)

17 Mia Hamm (1972)

18 Bonnie Blair (1964)

20 Lois Lowry (1937)
Bill Martin Jr. (1916)
Fred Rogers (1928)
Louis Sachar (1954)
David Suzuki (1936)

21 Rosie O'Donnell (1962)

22 Randolph Caldecott (1846)

25 Kate DiCamillo (1964)
Danica Patrick (1982)
Sheryl Swoopes (1971)

31 Al Gore (1948)

April

3 Amanda Bynes (1986)
Jane Goodall (1934)

4 Maya Angelou (1928)

5 Dean Kamen (1951)
Richard Peck (1934)
Colin Powell (1937)

7 Ronde Barber (1975)
Tiki Barber (1975)

8 Kofi Annan (1938)

10 David A. Adler (1947)

12 Beverly Cleary (1916)
Tony Hawk (1968)

15 Tim Duncan (1976)
Carol Greider (1961)
Emma Watson (1990)

16 Garth Williams (1912)

18 Melissa Joan Hart (1976)

25 Ella Fitzgerald (1917)

26 Patricia Reilly Giff (1935)

27 Ludwig Bemelmans (1898)
Coretta Scott King (1927)
Barbara Park (1947)

May

4 Don Wood (1945)

6 Judy Delton (1931)
Ted Lewin (1935)

10 Christopher Paul Curtis (1953)
Judith Jamison (1944)
Leo Lionni (1910)
Ellen Ochoa (1958)

11 Peter Sis (1949)

12 Betsy Lewin (1937)

14 Miranda Cosgrove (1993)
George Lucas (1944)
Emmitt Smith (1969)

16 Margret Rey (1906)

17 Gary Paulsen (1939)

20 Mary Pope Osborne (1949)

22 Arnold Lobel (1933)

23 Margaret Wise Brown (1910)

27 Rachel Carson (1907)

29 Andrew Clements (1949)

June

2 Freddy Adu (1989)
Anita Lobel (1934)

5 Rick Riordan (1964)
Richard Scarry (1919)

6 Tim Berners-Lee (1955)
Larisa Oleynik (1981)
Cynthia Rylant (1954)

9 Freddie Highmore (1992)

10 Tara Lipinski (1982)

Maurice Sendak (1928)

11 Joe Montana (1956)

13 Tim Allen (1953)

15 Jack Horner (1946)

18 Chris Van Allsburg (1949)

19 Aung San Suu Kyi (1945)

25 Eric Carle (1929)
Sonia Sotomayor (1955)

26 Derek Jeter (1974)
Michael Vick (1980)
Nancy Willard (1936)

30 Robert Ballard (1971)
Michael Phelps (1985)

July

2 Dave Thomas (1932)

6 George W. Bush (1946)

7 Michelle Kwan (1980)
Lisa Leslie (1972)

8 Jaden Smith (1998)

11 Patricia Polacco (1944)
E.B. White (1899)

12 Kristi Yamaguchi (1972)

13 Stephanie Kwolek (1923)

14 Laura Numeroff (1953)
Peggy Parish (1927)

18 Nelson Mandela (1918)

24 Barry Bonds (1964)
Mara Wilson (1987

26 Jan Berenstain (1923)

28 Natalie Babbitt (1932)

24 Jim Henson (1936)

25 Andrea Davis Pinkney (1963)

25 Will Smith (1968)

26 Serena Williams (1981)

28 Hilary Duff (1987)

29 Stan Berenstain (1923)

30 Dominique Moceanu (1981)

October

1 Mark McGwire (1963)

5 Grant Hill (1972
Maya Lin (1959)

6 Lonnie Johnson (1949)

7 Yo-Yo Ma (1955)

8 Faith Ringgold (1930)

9 Zachery Ty Bryan (1981)

10 James Marshall (1942)

11 Michelle Wie (1989)

12 Marion Jones (1975)

13 Nancy Kerrigan (1969)

17 Nick Cannon (1980)
Mae Jemison (1954)

18 Zac Efron (1987)
Wynton Marsalis (1961)

22 Ichiro Suzuki (1973)

23 Pele (1940)

24 Charlie White (1987)

25 Pedro Martinez (1971)

26 Regina Benjamin (1956)

Hillary Clinton (1947)
Steven Kellogg (1941)
Eric Rohmann (1957)

28 Bill Gates (1955)

31 Katherine Paterson (1932)

November

3 Janell Cannon (1957)

4 Laura Bush (1946)

5 Kevin Jonas (1987)

9 Lois Ehlert (1934)

12 Sammy Sosa (1968)

14 Astrid Lindgren (1907)
Condoleezza Rice (1954)
William Steig (1907)

15 Daniel Pinkwater (1941)

19 Savion Glover (1973)
Ken Griffey Jr. (1969)
Kerri Strug (1977)

20 Joe Biden (1942)

23 Miley Cyrus (1992)
Gloria Whelan (1923)

25 Marc Brown (1946)

26 Charles Schulz (1922)

27 Kevin Henkes (1960)
Bill Nye (1955)
Jaleel White (1977)

29 Louisa May Alcott (1832)
C.S. Lewis (1898)

Photo and Illustration Credits